FORBIDDEN MOUNTAIN

The FORBIDDEN MOUNTAIN

Christine Wright

Scripture Union
130 City Road, London EC1V 2NJ

By the same author:
(*for older readers*)
Turnabout
Coming Back
More than a Match

First published 1988

ISBN 0 86201 473 5

Phototypeset by Input Typesetting Ltd, London SW19 8DR
Printed and bound in Great Britain by Cox and Wyman Ltd, Reading

Thanks to Graham, Jenny and Alison who enjoyed the mountains with me

Chapter one

I slammed the back door very hard, stuffed my feet into my boots that always stood in the porch and ran down the rough and rocky garden.

'She wouldn't even listen to me!' I thought crossly. Usually I got on well with my mother, but that day we had had a big row, the first ever. I'd argued and argued, but she hadn't changed her mind – not even a little.

'Sorry, Jake,' she had said. 'I know why you don't like it, but it's not good shouting at me. We have decided.'

You see, my mother had just told me that she was going to get married again. My dad died when I was a little boy. Since then I'd lived alone with my mother and I was used to having her to myself. I was also used to having my own way a lot of the time. Now everything was changing.

I'd told my mum, 'But we're happy as we are!'

'Yes, Jake,' she had agreed, 'but I love Martin too. We want to be together and share our lives. I'm sure we'll all be happy.'

I didn't think so. As I ran to the end of the garden and squeezed through the fence, I was thinking it over. I liked Martin. I hope you don't think that I didn't. It wasn't that which upset me so much. Nor did I dislike his daughter, Holly, though I must admit I didn't like her that much either.

What really bothered me was that I felt my whole life would change for the worse. I still missed my dad, but, on the whole, I liked things just as they were. Why did Martin have to come and change it all?

I went for a long walk over the fields behind our house. Somewhere, I'm not sure where, those steep fields become the mountain. I walked a long way that day, but I didn't climb towards the mountain. I had promised my mother that I'd keep off the mountain. At that time, I really meant to keep the promise.

When I was small, my father had died there. He was part of a Mountain Rescue team. Quite often, he used to get calls to help people who'd got stranded in the hills. He was a superb climber, but, one night, in the cold and rain, he slipped. Normally, it would be stupid to go out at night in such weather, but he had to. It was his duty to rescue people in danger. You can die of exposure out on a mountain at night, so the team couldn't just wait until morning when the rescue would have been safer.

Usually, when my dad was called out, he came back within a few hours. That night, he didn't come back. He was killed in a terrible accident.

Now that you know how my father died, you'll understand why my mother had made me promise not to climb the mountain on my own.

So I stayed on the lower slopes not far from home. I never get tired of walking there. The ground is steep and rocky, broken by many little streams each with an unending supply of clear, gushing water. Watching the water cascade over the rocky beds of the streams is a pastime in itself. Angry and upset as I was that day, I found it soothing. I stopped to gaze before crossing each stream, brooding on the argument I'd had. I went over it a hundred times in my head.

'I'll do everything I can to change her mind,' I thought. 'I don't want a new father. I don't want a new sister. And I don't want to share my mother with anyone!'

We'd known Martin and Holly Stevens for quite a long time. They'd moved into a tiny cottage in our village a year or two before. We had met them at church. Since then, we'd done a lot of things together. Martin had a car and we didn't, so we often went to places that Mum and I couldn't have got to alone. In fact, we always had a good time when they were around. I always argued with Holly, though. She used to say such mean things. I couldn't help answering back! I used to call her 'Prickly' Holly. It suited her perfectly.

No, it wasn't that I hated Martin, nor even Holly really. I liked having them around, but not all the time! Why couldn't things stay just as they were?

I walked back nearly all the way home. It was spring time and the afternoon was only half gone. I decided to spend an hour in my hide.

My hide is a special kind of den and I must

tell you about it. It was a secret at the time. No one else in the world knew about it!

There are two fields just at the back of our house. They are divided by a sort of hedge which grows out of a ditch. In other parts of the country, I think, hedges are neat rows of bushes and trees. This hedge, where my hide is, is not a neat row at all. It has some small trees, oaks and birches, and windblown bushes, but it's mainly a tangle of branches and creepers. That's what makes it such a good place to hide – and not just for me. It's also a shelter for all kinds of plants and creatures.

In winter, there are birds using the hedge as a feeding place, taking the hawthorn and blackthorn berries and what they can eat of the creepers – the seeds and fruits. I expect birds flock there at night too, though I'm supposed to be indoors by dusk, so I don't see this myself. I do know that the hedge is one of the most sheltered places in the area. We have severe weather in winter, so I like to think of birds using the hedge as a roost.

The fields either side of the hedge are used in winter. The farmer doesn't let the young sheep out onto the mountain for their first winter. He keeps them in the lower pastures to harden up. Then, in spring, he brings down the older ewes for lambing. The younger ones go up onto the mountain to graze as soon as the weather's mild enough.

Then, quite suddenly, it seems, the hedge comes alive. All winter it has looked dead, just branches and rotting vegetation. In spring it lives again, leaves and flowers feathering out from tight buds in just a few days. Flowers poke through the leaf litter along the hedge, first the odd primrose, then cowslips, later celandines and many others.

I know summer is really coming when the first butterflies flutter across the field. Beetles, spiders and flies appear from nowhere. How these insects survive the freezing winter I don't know, but they come out with the warm weather and make the hedge their home. In the empty fields the flowers and grass grow unchecked with the sheep gone. There's so much to write about in my notebook.

Autumn arrives and the bracken on the hillside turns brown. In the hedge the leaves colour red, yellow or brown, then drop. The berries give a splash of colour too. The field looks trampled as the grass withers and is laden with droplets of dew which don't dry all day. The flowers, even sturdy parsleys, die and droop.

Then winter comes again. And I spend less time in the hide and more tramping about the lower slopes and hills looking for buzzards and harriers.

It was spring at the time I'm telling you about. I'd been away from my hide for a while because I'd been busy with exams at school. Now I was glad to be back!

The only way into the hide was between the creepers. I had to crawl on my knees and elbows down into the ditch out of which the hedge grew. Up out of the ditch a little was a flat, rocky platform. From there I could see across both the fields as far as the mountain. I could also see most of what happened in the hedge itself.

I always got my notebook from under one of the rocks as soon as I arrived. It was wrapped in plastic. I couldn't help rustling a bit as I got it out, but after that I used to sit completely still and watch. There was just enough room to sit up among the branches or to lie down flat, completely hidden.

I arrived that day feeling unhappy, but I soon forgot about it! Through the tangle of creepers, not far from my hide, I could see that a blackbird had made a nest in the hedge. She chirped in alarm when I arrived, so I lay still for a while, then edged forward so carefully that she stayed on the nest. I could tell it was the female blackbird. She had dull brown feathers, unlike the black male.

I watched. I didn't try to remove my notebook. I sat as still as I could. I wondered how long the bird had been there. How long would it be before the eggs hatched? Would I be able to see the baby birds?

It drove out of my mind all my troubles. When I left the hide (very slowly, of course) as it became dark, I felt quite cheerful. I squeezed through the fence into our garden and saw that the light was already shining in the kitchen window. That meant that tea was on its way!

Chapter two

The next day, Sunday, Martin and Holly were coming to have lunch with us. It was a mad rush to get out to church! My mum's not very good at getting up early. She had to dash about trying to do everything at once.

I didn't offer to help. I'd promised myself that I'd do all I could to stop my mum getting married again. I thought that being moody was a good way to do it! I suppose I hoped that my mum would say, 'If you're so miserable, Jake, I won't marry Martin after all'. Of course, she didn't. All that happened was that we both ended up being unhappy.

We left for church in a great hurry. We always went there on Sundays, unless one of us was ill. When my dad was alive (and just after he died), we used to talk about God and pray together quite often. Later, when I got a bit older, I began to feel embarrassed about it. Mum stopped suggesting things like reading the Bible and praying. I never forgot about God, though, nor did my mum. To be honest, though, I didn't talk to God much. I only remembered him properly in emergencies, when I needed help, except, of course, on Sundays.

We met Martin and Holly at church as usual. Lately, we'd sat with them every week. That day we arrived just in time. I ended up sitting next to Holly.

She is younger than me. At that time she had long, loose hair, fair like Martin's and she always wore, not just for best, but all the time, pretty, brightly coloured dresses, usually red or green. She looked very sweet, like a pretty doll, but she was never sweet with me.

'Late again, Jake,' she whispered.

'Just in time, Holly,' I gasped. (We'd run most of the way!)

'We've been here ages,' she boasted. 'We helped put out the chairs.'

I was thinking up a really crushing reply, but Martin leant forward frowning at us for making a noise. I glared at her and turned away.

I like the services at our church. There's always something to think about. When I'm unhappy or fed up about things, I usually go out feeling better. It happened that day.

I'd been dreading being with Martin and Holly that day. And I knew I'd been horrible to my mother. During the prayers, I began to feel sorry for being so difficult and unkind. I wanted to be different.

Later, there was a reading from the Bible. There was something in it about 'serving each other' which stuck in my mind. I just couldn't stop thinking about it.

I suppose that 'serving each other' means that you should try to help other people. You shouldn't just be thinking about yourself. Instead, you should forget what you want yourself and look for ways to do things for everyone else.

Doesn't that seem a very hard thing to do? In my case, it would have meant forgetting how I felt about Mum getting married. I'd have had to think about how the others felt! I was sure that I couldn't do that! Somehow, though, I knew I shouldn't go on being moody and selfish.

So, this is what I made up my mind to do. If I couldn't get my own way, I'd just keep myself to myself. I'd give up trying to make other people unhappy. I'd keep quiet about my feelings. I reckoned that would be good enough.

On the way home I said nothing. I thought, 'If I speak, I'll say the wrong thing and upset someone.'

But, trust Holly, she said, 'Jake's grumpy!'

'We noticed,' my mother said. (You'd have thought she'd have stood up for me!)

Martin said, 'I expect he's got things on his mind, Holly. Leave him alone.'

Holly is no good at leaving people alone. She had a try, turned her back on me and stared out of the car window. Just a few seconds later, though, she said, 'Can we get out that game this afternoon, Jake? You know, the one with the castles and dragons?'

I scowled, 'You can have it out, but don't expect me to play it, will you?'

She screwed up her nose and pulled a mean face. I turned away, cross with myself. After all that I decided earlier, I'd upset Holly already!

'Actually, Holly,' said Martin before she could say anything more, 'I was hoping to have a talk with Jake this afternoon. I'm sure that you and

Sue will find lots to do together.'

My mother said, 'What a good idea!' I could tell they'd planned it all before. They'd set it up so that Martin could talk me into being pleased about the wedding.

'Shall we take a walk up the mountain, Jake?' he asked. And, of course, I agreed. I never miss a chance like that.

Martin drove the car far up the twisting mountain road, then parked on a patch of ground near a steep climb into a bleak, rugged part of the mountain. In summer, this place is seething with people. Some come just to look. They stand by their cars, gazing up at the rocky sides of the mountain that loom over them, or gazing down at the hills and lakes below. Some come to climb the sheer walls of rock, inching their way up roped to each other. Others are there to walk the same path that we took that day. It is steep, but not difficult and leads to the summit.

That day it was too early for many visitors. The weather was still doubtful, quite cold and very windy, and we were the only people there. After making a few checks of the weather and the equipment we were carrying, Martin said we could make a start. 'We'll just climb to the first ridge,' he said. 'We'd better keep well below the snow.'

The snow had been lying as a white cap on the mountain all winter. Now it was melting fast. In a few weeks it would have gone altogether and the summit would be bare rock again.

We walked side by side up the well-marked track that twisted between huge humps of rock, sometimes crossing cascades of icy water bubbling down from the snow cap. Later, the track narrowed and we were walking between sheer walls of granite, often without a view of the ridge ahead.

I went on in silence. Soon I had left Martin far behind and out of sight. I knew that my father must have come this way often. Surely *he* hadn't had to keep stopping to catch his breath! So I worked hard to keep myself going. My legs ached. My heart was pounding. My breaths were hard and short. I pushed myself on. I didn't stop once until I was standing on the first ridge. That's where I had to stop because Martin had said so, but I knew I could have gone further!

I stood looking back the way I'd come. Martin was not even in sight yet. I was glad. It was utterly quiet and lonely up there. Far from the roads, far from anyone else, far from the rest of the world, I was alone. I loved it.

From that side of the mountain, I couldn't see our valley. Looking down over unfamiliar streams and lakes, over someone else's stone-built village, over different roads that you don't know, is far less interesting. I'd never climbed so near the summit before, but it didn't give me the thrill that I'd have got if I'd been able to spot the fields, the buildings, the streets that I knew so well from another angle.

Even so, when a bright orange dot appeared from around a rock below, I was sorry. It was Martin. I wouldn't be alone much longer.

'My dad would never have been left behind like that,' I thought. 'He'd have led all the way up.'

I'd always liked Martin before. But now he wanted to spoil my life, I couldn't help thinking nasty thoughts about him. I couldn't stop myself.

I shouted, 'Where have you been, then?' It was meant to be hurtful, but he smiled. He was too breathless to shout back. When he got near enough to make me hear without yelling, he said, 'Jake, you certainly take after your father!' He clambered up a few more steps, then sat down on a flat rock. 'You came up there like a true mountaineer!'

Why did he want to talk about my dad? I'd have thought he'd want me to forget him!

'My dad was always on the mountains,' I said proudly. 'He rescued thousands of people.' (I didn't really know how many. I said 'thousands' to show Martin how much I admired my dad. I wanted Martin to feel feeble.)

He was quiet for a moment. I hoped that he was feeling bad about what I'd said. He was rubbing the hairs in his fair beard thoughtfully.

'Jake,' he said at last, 'I never knew your dad. I know how brave he was. Everyone speaks well of him. I hope you'll go on loving him and being proud of him – always.'

I was very surprised.

'Perhaps you think I'm trying to take his place,' he went on. 'I'm not, Jake. I know how you feel about him. That's good. I don't want to change it. All I want is to be your friend.'

I looked away. I thought, 'If he wants to be my friend, why is he trying to change everything?' I didn't say so, though.

'Will you try to accept what's happening?' he asked. 'I know it must be hard, but will you try? It's not for me, Jake, but for Sue, your mother. Try to make her happy.'

I nodded and forced a tiny smile.

There was tomato soup and toast for tea. Holly couldn't stop talking about what she'd been doing all afternoon. I don't think anyone noticed how quiet I was.

After tea Martin said, 'When we are living together as a family, we'll want to pray together, won't we? Why don't we start now? We've had a good day. Let's thank God for it.'

I began to feel awkward. I glanced at my mum, hoping she'd give some excuse to stop it. She was looking at me. 'I'd like that,' she said.

Holly said, 'Daddy and I have a prayer time every day.'

I was on my own, then. I gave in. 'All right,' I said grudgingly.

I must admit that it wasn't too bad. I don't know now what I was afraid of. I suppose I thought I'd have to pray out loud and feel silly about it, but that didn't happen. I found that you can pray just as well in your thoughts. It was a long time since I'd talked to God about ordinary things. It was great to tell him how I was feeling.

'Father God,' I said privately to him, 'I want us to be happy – all of us. At the moment, I'm very unhappy. I don't want things to change. Please don't let Martin and Holly come and live here. I know I'll hate it if they do.'

Chapter three

I remember the next day, Monday, for two reasons. One was that I was so helpful at home that my mother just couldn't believe it. I tidied my bedroom without being asked. I cleaned Mum's shoes and my own before school and helped in the kitchen.

I thought that if my mum could get out to work every day without rushing, she wouldn't want to marry Martin. It seems stupid now, but I thought it might work! Anyway, she left in plenty of time that morning, saying how glad she was that I'd been so kind. So we both felt happy, but for different reasons.

The other reason for remembering that day is that it was the last time I went to my hide before it stopped being a secret.

I used to come home earlier than Mum. As usual, she'd left out something for me to eat. I changed my clothes and went down the garden, through the gap in the fence and ran across the field to the hedge.

I wriggled very gently into the hide, stopping every time I heard the chirping noise that blackbirds make when they're alarmed. Then I sat still for a long time, although it wasn't very warm that day. I was hoping to get a glimpse of the eggs in the nest, though I didn't want to disturb the bird in case she didn't come back.

As I sat I could see the outline of the mountain clear against the sky. Sometimes the mist is so low that there is nothing to see, just as though there's no mountain at all, but that day I could see every detail from the grassy slopes to the rocky summit.

A view of a mountain is always changing. The colours are never the same. It changes from day to day. Sometimes, as it was that day, it is a green and grey mountain, splashes of yellow gorse showing it is spring at last. It stands clear and sharp, so that I can follow the line of each stone wall that runs across it. Other days, usually early in the morning, there's a pink tinge to it, and, when the sky is heavy, the mountain is dark and gloomy, cascades of water showing up like specks of cotton wool. Colours change from season to season too. Patches of flowering heather mean it's summer; brown means the bracken has finished its life and it's autumn; dull green and grey and the winter is ahead; white and the bitterest weather has arrived; lighter green and yellow gorse flowering and the cycle of seasons has begun again.

I always wished that I was allowed to climb even half way to the summit on my own, even just to the highest stone wall above me. I wanted to make it more my own mountain, to explore it properly. Looking at it from below was not good enough. I wanted to be up there very often like the farmers were, until I knew it in every mood, every weather, every season.

The blackbird did not move at all while I was there. I didn't see her mate, though I did see a pair of stonechats passing backwards and forwards. I recognise these birds because they have unusual pinkish chestnut feathers beneath and dark brown above. The male has a white collar and there's a flash of white on the wings. Also stonechats make funny jerky movements with their wings as they land. I love listening to their chattering call. It sounds like pebbles rubbing together.

When it began to get dark, I eased my way out of the hide and went home. My mother had already cooked our supper. We sat together eating and talking. We used to enjoy those evenings together, just the two of us. After supper I did my homework and Mum wrote letters. Getting married seems to mean a lot of letter writing. I didn't ask why. I didn't want to talk about the wedding.

It was getting late when I finished my homework, but my mother was still writing and the supper things were still on the table.

'I'll clear the table,' I said.

Mum hardly looked up. 'Good,' she said.

As I piled up the plates I thought, 'She's more interested in her letter than in me.' And I began to blame Martin for that because she'd have had plenty of time to give to me if it hadn't been for him.

'I'll show Mum that we don't need him!' I thought as I went out to the kitchen. So I worked vigorously and cleared up in no time. I polished every plate and cup, shone every saucepan, scrubbed the table and even swept the floor.

Looking back I can see that what I was trying to do was pointless. At the time, though, I did believe that I could change my mother's plans by being helpful. I'd even thought of several jobs that I could do and was planning to start on them in the morning.

Then my mother came out. 'Oh Jake,' she cried in amazement, 'you have worked hard. Thank you!'

I stood there beaming. I was proud of myself. I thought she ought to repay me by saying she wouldn't get married. How stupid I was!

'Martin will be pleased about this,' she went on (and my smile dropped). 'He doesn't think you pull your weight around the house, you know. But this will change his mind!'

'I didn't do it for Martin,' I growled.

'I know. I know.' She saw she'd upset me. 'I only meant that it'll be easier – when we're all living together – if you're willing to do more.'

That made me furious. It had all gone wrong. This wasn't what I wanted her to say! I shouted, 'You'll never catch me helping again. Never!'

I ran upstairs and slammed my bedroom door. After I'd banged about for a while, I sat on the edge of my bed. I was thinking about my prayer. I'd asked God to stop Martin and Holly coming to live with us, but he hadn't given me the answer I'd wanted.

'I'll never change Mum's mind,' I thought. 'I just know I'll be miserable for the rest of my life.'

I was horrible for days. My mother couldn't

understand why and didn't know how to help me. I knew I was making her sad, but I was too selfish to change it. What's more, it rained so much that I was stuck indoors and couldn't go to my hide. On top of that, Holly was invited to come and stay during the week, her first visit on her own. She was going to sleep in the spare room while Martin was away from home.

I scowled at her and at Martin when they arrived with her suitcase, but she was too excited to notice.

'It's going to be much better than when I have to stay with Mrs Jones,' she said. 'Her house is so old and gloomy and she makes me go to bed so early!'

Martin said, 'But she's always been very kind to you. Remember what I said about calling in to see her while I'm away. She loves having visitors now that she can't get out.'

Holly pulled the most terrible face. Martin didn't see, but I did – and I couldn't help grinning. She looked so funny. It was impossible to carry on being sulky after that, at least with Holly. I smiled at her. She smiled back and we began to talk, mostly about how awful it was at Mrs Jones's. I refused to talk to Martin, though.

Then, while my mother was taking Holly up to the spare room, Martin said to me, 'Jake, you are making Sue so unhappy. I never thought you'd be so tiresome.'

I just turned away, but he was not having that!

'Look, Jake,' he went on, 'this won't do. Sue and I are getting married and the sooner you accept it the better.'

Isn't it surprising how people sometimes say exactly the wrong thing? 'You can't force me to,' I told him.

'I don't want to,' he said. 'I just want you to try and understand.'

I wouldn't listen. I didn't want to understand. I just wanted someone to understand me!

After he'd gone, my mother said, 'I've got to sort out Holly's room, Jake. Can you find something to do together for a while?'

I looked at Holly and she looked at me. There was still a long time before supper – almost an hour. What was I supposed to do with her for all that time?

I don't think we'd ever been left together like that before, not unless we were already doing something. I didn't know what to say. For once, she said nothing. I think she was suddenly missing her dad. I was afraid she'd start crying. I got scared.

'Do what you like,' I said. 'I'm going out.'

I ran to the back door and slammed it behind me. I heard her wail, 'Jake!' I was thrusting my feet into my boots as fast as I could. I heard her again saying, 'Jake! Wait!', but I didn't wait. I ran faster down the garden, through the fence and across the field. Soon I was lying on the muddy ground, wriggling into the hide.

A little later I heard rustling, the snapping of twigs, scuffling noises. Sometimes a rabbit would come close to the hedge making sounds like that, though much softer. This sounded like a thousand rabbits together. Soon I heard that same wail, 'Jake!' I turned crossly and the blackbird flew off her nest chirping in alarm. That made me crosser, although it had been me, not Holly, who'd disturbed her. Yet I stayed where I was, hoping that Holly couldn't see me.

I could see her. Her dress was bright red. She was trying to climb through the hedge where it was tangly and twiggy. Suddenly, there was a little scream.

'Jake!' she squealed. 'Help me!' I didn't move. 'Please,' she added.

She sounded so pitiful that I had to go. I clambered out quickly. It didn't matter how much noise I made now that the blackbird had gone. I stomped through the dead bracken.

'What are you doing here?' I shouted. 'This is my place.'

'My hair's caught,' she sobbed.

'It'd serve you right if I left you there,' I yelled. 'No one's allowed here but me.'

'I didn't know,' she sniffed. 'You said I could do what I liked.'

Well, that was true, of course, but I said, 'Why did you follow me?'

'I wanted to. Jake, please help me. I'm stuck.' She pulled at her fair hair which was caught around some branches. I don't know how it got in such a mess. It took ages to free her.

'Lucky for you your dad's away,' I said as I worked at the knot.

'Why?' she squeaked. I was trying not to hurt her, but sometimes I did.

'You're in such a mess,' I said. 'He'd go mad if he saw you like that.'

'I know,' she sobbed. Her dress was torn and her legs were scratched and dirty. My mother never complained about me getting muddy or my clothes torn, but Martin used to worry a lot about how Holly looked. He was always warning her about being careful. I remember how he told her off one day when she grazed her cheek on a wall. I could just imagine what he'd say if he saw the state she was in now.

I began to feel sorry for her. A sad, frightened Holly was nothing like the prickly, spiteful Holly that I was used to. I finished untangling her hair, then, to cheer her up, I said, 'Swear you'll never tell anyone and I'll show you my hide.'

With a sniff she replied, 'I know where it is already.'

What happened next I can't really tell. I was just about to make a terrible threat like, 'If you ever tell anyone, I'll cut all your hair off'. I nearly did, but I didn't actually say it. I think it was the first time I'd ever stopped myself doing something wrong in quite that way. I suppose that God was already working in my life, getting me ready for what was going to happen. I didn't know that at the time, though. I only knew that I was going to threaten Holly – and then thought of something better to say.

'Look, Holly, my hide is a secret. You won't go and tell about it, will you? It'll be spoilt if everyone knows.'

'I won't say a word!' she promised, her eyes shining.

I believed her. It was much nicer than getting the same promise by frightening her.

I showed Holly the hide. I told her how to creep in on your hands and knees, pushing your way through the long, woody creepers. She followed me into the usual place half way up the slope into the ditch, deep inside the tangled branches. I showed her the way to sit so that you kept on the stones and didn't slide into the mud.

'See the nest?' I asked, pointing out the rounded nest of grass and twigs just visible several metres away. 'There must be eggs in it. I've seen the blackbirds sitting on it. We mustn't stay long now. They'll come back when we've gone, I hope.'

I'd always thought I'd hate sharing the hide, but I enjoyed showing her everything. She listened to all I had to say. She was especially interested in my notebook.

'Why don't you draw the things you see?' she asked.

I explained that it would take too long, but she said she'd show me how to sketch quickly. I wasn't sure about letting her draw in my notebook. Instead I let her use a spare page in the back.

'See?' she said after only a few seconds.

I was impressed. She'd drawn one of the bluebells that were starting to open just in front of us.

'Next time you come,' I promised, 'you can draw something in the front.'

What a surprise that afternoon was! I'd done so many things I'd never dreamt of doing!

When we got back to the house, I even asked my mother if Holly could have some of my old clothes to wear while she was staying. 'They need to be dark green or brown or grey,' I said.

Mum took one look at the mess Holly was in

and agreed. 'If you're going to be out with Jake,' she said, 'the older and tougher the clothes you wear, the better. I'll plait your hair back too. It'll be out of your way.'

I smiled at Holly. I hadn't told my mother why we needed camouflage colours and Holly kept quiet about it too. I'd been right to trust her. It was funny how much I was starting to like her.

Chapter four

The first day of Holly's visit turned out to be good, and things continued well. Down in the hide after school, we got to know each other better. We didn't talk much, but I began to trust her to be very quiet and still. I found out that she's keen on wild life like me. She knows the names of far more plants than I do. The big difference between us is that I've had to learn most of what I know out of books, while Holly has learnt a lot from Martin.

We kept a watch on the blackbird's nest. I was glad that she had returned after I'd frightened her off and we were waiting for the eggs to hatch. Once we saw the bird turning the eggs. At least, that's what we guessed she was doing. We wrote it all down in the notebook. Holly drew the nest surrounded by hawthorn blossom.

Then, at the weekend, things changed. I didn't mind sharing my hide with Holly, but I definitely did not want her with me all the time. On Saturday morning she wanted to come and play football with me.

I said, 'You can't come. It's only for boys.'

My mother said, 'Now that's not fair, Jake. Holly's only here for a week. There's no harm in her coming to watch.'

I won't go into the long argument we had after that. I lost. Holly tagged along and I hated it.

I suppose I could have been rude to her in front of all my friends, just to show them that I hadn't wanted her there. But, as I've explained, God had been working on me and I thought how hurt she'd have been. So I put up with all the jeering and the jokes against me because I'd brought a girl with me. It spoilt the game for me, though. I made Holly stay off the pitch while we played by promising her I'd play football with her in the garden in the afternoon. I wasn't in a very good mood afterwards, I can tell you. I reckoned Holly had ruined my whole day.

I was feeling so sorry for myself that I forgot my earlier feelings. The nasty side of me had come back and I sulked over lunch.

Afterwards, I crept out of the house quietly so that no one would hear me. I used the front door and sneaked up the passage beside the house to the back porch. Mum was making so much noise with the saucepans in the kitchen that she didn't hear me putting on my boots. I hoped that Holly hadn't noticed that I was missing. I stopped at the end of the garden and stood for a moment, wondering if I'd hear her chasing me. No, all was quiet. I was free!

At the time, I didn't feel bad about breaking my promise to Holly. I was just glad to have some time to myself. What was I going to do with it?

There was no point in going to the hide. Holly would soon find me there. Nor could I go and see any of my friends, not after what had happened that morning. I glanced up. The mountain stretched before me, inviting me. I knew it was wrong, but I'd just broken one promise to Holly and breaking another didn't seem too bad just at that moment.

I decided to climb the mountain.

Our side of the mountain belongs to Mr Grainger. His sheep live up there most of the time, eating the rough grass they find. Every year he drives them down for dipping, for shearing, to choose those he wants to sell and, in spring, for lambing. Most of the ewes had had their lambs already, but they were still down in the fields near the farmhouse where he could keep an eye on them. As I began to climb I could hear the high wailing bleats of the lambs and the low answers of the ewes. As I got higher I could look down and see them all as white and grey splodges on the rocky fields. After a while I could no longer see the sheep and their cries seemed distant.

Now the ground was more littered with rocks than before. There was some sparse grass and tiny wild flowers among patches of boggy moss that squelched under my feet. The dead bracken, still its autumn brown, had curls of new green growth just showing from underneath.

From time to time I'd see another stone wall ahead of me. I set my mind on climbing from one wall to another without stopping. Most of these dry stone walls aren't used any more. They were built by hand centuries ago. Some are repaired by the farmers, but others just stand, toppling this way and that where the wind and rain have pushed them.

It was a hard climb. My lungs felt as if they were burning. My feet began to feel like heavy weights. I didn't stop, though, except for a few minutes at each wall. And at each stop the world below was smaller and the mountain ahead was even vaster.

I knew the proper way to walk uphill. My dad taught me when I was a little boy and I've never forgotten. You should take short, even steps, keep upright and use your legs, not your hands and arms, to pull you up. I knew that it was less tiring once you were used to it, but the ache in my legs made me long to rest them. I wouldn't. I wanted to be an expert walker and climber like my father. I had to train hard.

The ground was getting steeper and steeper. At last I reached the last tumble-down wall and had to make up my mind what to do next.

There was still a very long, hard climb to the summit over dangerous, empty ground. I'd never come so high before, except from the other side with Martin. In the last few days the heavy rain had washed all but a few traces of snow from the top of the mountain. It had a bare, rocky head, but, even so, I knew that it would be difficult to get there.

I glanced at my watch and guessed that I would have time to climb all the way as long as I came down quickly afterwards. I'd be home in time for tea if all went well.

Half of me wanted to go further. Here I was, all alone, making my dream come true – the dream of getting to the summit. I knew I could do it. Despite the pain I'd had getting as far as I had, I was sure I had the strength to go on. All I had to do, if I chose, was to press one foot, then the other, against the firm rock of the mountain, and I'd get what I'd always wanted. I'd reach the top! I imagined standing up there, head in the sky, the rest of the world lying before me – and nowhere further to go!

The other half of me was thinking of home. Down there in one of those granite and slate houses was my mother. I was remembering how I'd solemnly promised her that I'd never climb the mountain – not even this far. Without taking another step upwards, I was breaking my promise. I didn't like to think of myself as untrustworthy. I was ashamed.

So, I stood there arguing with myself. Then, slowly and sadly, I began to climb down. The thrill had gone out of the adventure. I should never have gone in the first place.

My mother never used to ask me where I'd been. I didn't want to admit to her what I'd done, but I couldn't look her in the eye when I got home. Also, she soon reminded me of my other broken promise.

'Jake, didn't you tell Holly you'd play with her this afternoon?'

I said, 'I might have done.'

'She's been looking for you, though.'

'Sorry,' I said. I didn't mean it. It just seemed the quickest way of ending the conversation.

'I hope you'll make it up to her, then,' she said.

She had that new tone of exasperation in her voice. I glanced up at her. She was looking at me as if she hardly knew me, frowning as though she couldn't understand me, wisps of brown hair across her puzzled face. I hated it.

I mumbled something which might have sounded like, 'All right,' and went off quickly. I hoped to avoid Holly for a while. I felt bad about what I'd done, but was too selfish to actually 'make it up to her'.

She must have heard me. No sooner had I closed my bedroom door than she was knocking and calling me, 'Jake!'

I pretended not to hear, hoping she'd go away, but she began to open the door. I leapt up and slammed it in her face.

'Jake!' she squealed. 'Let me come in!'

'No,' I replied, leaning against the door.

'I want to tell you something.'

'I don't want to hear.'

'Please, it's important. You've got to listen.'

'No, I haven't,' I said. 'I've got my fingers in my ears.'

So she shouted. She doesn't give in easily. 'Don't listen, then, but you won't have a hide any more. It's going to be pulled down!'

I was trying to work out whether she meant it or whether she was making it up.

Holly banged the door. 'Are you listening now? Your hide is going to be pulled down unless we do something. And we can't do something unless you LISTEN!'

I was listening. I opened the door a crack.

'What do you mean?' I asked.

Her face was red from shouting. 'I heard them when I was in the hide,' she told me. 'I was looking for you, but you weren't there, but I stayed and I was sitting still when – oh Jake, guess what? The eggs have hatched. I saw the blackbirds taking food into the nest. I didn't see the baby birds, though.'

I opened the door and let her in.

'Then,' Holly went on when I'd shut the door again, 'the parent birds flew off suddenly and I saw two men coming over the field. I heard what they were saying. Guess what?'

'Go on,' I said impatiently.

Her eyes grew large. 'One said, "It's thick enough – a couple of days' labour".'

'What did he mean?' I asked.

'Pull the hedge down,' she explained, 'because the other one said, "I could grub it out myself in less time." Then the other one said, "Not with all those roots. No point in leaving all the stumps to grow again." '

I sat on my bed dumbfounded. 'Are you sure, Holly?' I said at last.

She nodded. 'What are we going to do, Jake?'

I didn't know. 'Was one a big, red-faced man with black hair?' I asked.

'Yes, and the other – '

'Never mind him. The one that matters is Mr Grainger. He's the farmer who owns the field. We've got to stop him.'

'How?' she asked.

'Somehow,' I said.

As we sat side by side in thought, I began to realise just what Holly had done. If she'd been different, she would have paid me back for breaking my promise by keeping the news to herself. Instead, she'd come to me as a friend after I'd been unkind to her.

'I'm sorry I went off without you,' I said.

'Good thing you did,' she replied. 'Otherwise we'd have been playing football and I wouldn't have been in the hide at the right time. Good thing I was wearing your old clothes too or they'd have seen me.'

Isn't that amazing! She'd forgiven me already. I think Holly's much nicer than me really.

Chapter five

'How can we go and see Mrs Jones as well?' asked Holly the next afternoon.

We were walking along the road together. Our plan had been to walk up to Mr Grainger's house, but as we were leaving, my mother had said, 'While you're out, why not pop into Mrs Jones's house? She'd be so pleased to see you.' Of course, we hadn't told her why we were going out, so we had sort of promised that we would visit the old woman who used to look after Holly.

'We haven't got time,' I told Holly. 'Mrs Jones can wait for another day.' I knew how far it was to Mr Grainger's if you went by road. It was quicker across the fields, but this was a proper visit, a serious one. I thought we ought to go up to the house from the road.

Holly was bothered. 'Dad did tell me to visit Mrs Jones while he was away,' she said.

'We'll go tomorrow after school, then.'

'But we told Sue we'd go today,' she went on.

'Look,' I said impatiently. 'We can only do one thing or the other. Which are you going to do? I'm going to the farm. I don't care what you do!'

It wasn't very fair of me. I'd promised to look after Holly and she knew she was supposed to stay with me. Mrs Jones lived at the other end of the village, so Holly would have had a long walk on her own if she'd decided to go.

'I'll come to the farm,' she said, but as we walked on she added, 'I wish we hadn't said we'd go to see Mrs Jones, though.'

So did I, especially if it meant that Holly was going to be a drag all afternoon. We had to walk about a mile after we'd left the village. It's only a small road with no footpaths on either side. For a while we walked in single file. I went first, Holly trailing behind. Every so often I had to stop and wait for her.

'Hurry up!' I'd say and she'd quicken her pace for a few steps, then slow down again. It is a steep climb along that road, but it wasn't that which made Holly slow.

'Look, Holly,' I said at last, 'we've got to save the hedge, haven't we? We didn't exactly promise to go and see Mrs Jones, did we? We only said we'd think about it. And we have, haven't we?'

'I suppose so,' she said unhappily.

'Maybe there'll be time on the way home,' I suggested, though I was sure there wouldn't.

Anyway, she brightened.

'We won't get into trouble anyway,' I told her. 'Mum never asks where I've been.'

'Are you sure?' she asked.

'Definite,' I told her.

She smiled and cheered up, and we began to make better progress. The road circles round Mr Grainger's land on one side and another farm on the other. You seem to be walking around the edge of the mountain, for, however far on you go towards the farmhouse, the mountain is always the same distance away to your right.

On either side of the road is a dry stone wall. They are kept in perfect repair because they keep the livestock off the roads when these bottom fields are being used. I've watched the farmers rebuilding these walls. It's all done using the natural stones and rocks lying on the ground. They don't use cement, but choose each stone to fit the place where it's needed, just like finding the right piece in a jigsaw puzzle. It's the way the stones balance that counts. I've tried to do it myself, but it's not as easy as it looks! My wall fell down.

As we walked along that afternoon, Holly and I were talking about the walls. I explained about building them and she told me the names of some of the plants growing in the crevices between the stones.

'I've seen birds nesting in the walls too,' I told her. 'They were wheaters. I recognised them by their white rumps. I'll show you where it was one day.'

'I think our hedge makes a better home,' Holly said. 'Much more comfortable.'

'It won't be a good home at all if we don't change Mr Grainger's mind,' I reminded her.

'He will listen, won't he?' she asked.

'I don't know,' I told her, 'but we've got to try and make him. We've got to explain how important the hedge is.'

We crossed the cattle grid that took us up the track onto Mr Grainger's farm. There was still a long, steep climb to the house. The track had gates across it every so often, but Holly and I didn't bother to open and close them. Instead we climbed every one. I'd been climbing gates all my life, but it was something new to Holly. You may find that hard to believe, but she had never been out much without her dad. He was always scared in case she hurt herself or tore her dress or got frightened at the top!

I remember once, when we were all out together, my mother had said, 'For heaven's sake, Martin, don't worry so much. Holly's not a china doll!'

In fact, he didn't need to fuss over her at all. She was perfectly all right climbing those gates. In my old trousers, she was free and could get over quite easily, though a bit slowly. I was anxious to get on, but I didn't try to hurry her. She was having such a good time!

The nearer we got to the house, the more noisy it became. The fields were full of ewes and lambs calling to each other. We saw Mr Grainger in one of the fields, so we didn't have to go up to the house in the end. He was looking after one of the sheep, so we stopped leaning over the gate, and watched. We weren't sure whether to call or not, so we just waited to see if he'd notice us.

I never get tired of watching lambs. They're so funny. They leap around, full of bounce, but always stay close to their own mothers. I don't know how they know which is which, but they seem to. Every lamb can find his mother easily. He pushes into her side and begins to suck, his shaking tail telling you how much he enjoys the milk she gives!

All Mr Grainger's sheep, except the lambs, are marked with a red 'T' in the centre of their backs. This is so that he knows which are his when he drives them down from the mountain. It's quite common for other sheep to get mixed up with his when they're wandering about looking for food. He sends the strays back to their owners whose land joins up with his.

Mr Grainger had been bending over a sheep for some time before he straightened up and saw us.

Holly whispered, 'I think that sheep's dead.'

My heart gave a thud, because I hate to think of animals dying or even being ill. I glanced again at the sheep. It was lying perfectly still, its head thrown back in an odd way. Holly called out, 'Is it dead, Mr Grainger?'

He glanced back and then walked towards us. 'It happens,' he said. 'I usually lose one or two at lambing.'

'That's terrible,' Holly cried accusingly. 'You ought to get the vet out or something!'

I didn't think that was very sensible. After all, we'd come to try and change Mr Grainger's mind about the hedge. It'd do no good making him angry before we started.

'Mr Grainger,' I said quickly, 'can we have a talk – if you're not too busy?'

He looked at me for a few seconds. 'Collier's boy, isn't it?' he asked.

I nodded. He'd seen me often before. I used to watch him and his men working. He'd never talked to me before, though. 'I'm Jake Collier,' I said. 'This is Holly. She's going to be my sister.'

He looked at Holly as he had looked at me, but before he had time to say anything, she asked, 'Are you truly going to pull our hedge out?'

He didn't answer quickly, just looked for a while.

'Which hedge would that be?' he asked.

He must have known. There was only one place on his land with a hedge, but Holly explained anyway where it was.

'Who says I'm going to pull any hedge out?' he asked. He had been friendly, but suddenly he seemed angry.

'I – I heard somewhere – ' Holly said with a blush. She was still keeping the secret about the hide, you see.

'Well, you keep your nose out of my concerns,' he snapped.

Holly went redder still. I said, 'We don't know if it's true, but we thought we ought to tell you that it's a wildlife habitat. All sorts of plants and creatures live there. There are birds nesting in it right now.'

Mr Grainger's face was always red, weather beaten, but it grew dark and angry. 'You've been talking to some of those "conservation" people, have you? These people who think you can run a farm by looking after birds and insects? It's not that easy, Jake Collier. You go back and tell them I have to feed my family and look after my home. How do they think butterflies and bees pay my bills? You go and ask them that!'

'We haven't been talking to anyone!' protested Holly.

Mr Grainger didn't hear. 'You go back the way you came!' he shouted, pointing down the track. 'You tell whoever it is who's sent you that I'll run my farm my own way!'

We didn't know what to say. I'd wanted to ask him why he had to destroy the hedge, but it didn't seem the right time to ask. 'Come on,' I told Holly, taking her hand which was clinging tightly to the fence. For a while, she just went on staring at the farmer.

'Go on,' he yelled. She let go and held onto me. 'Mind your own business in future!' he called after us.

We walked down the hill, feeling shocked.

'He wasn't very nice,' Holly said in a shaky voice. 'Why did he say we'd been talking to someone?'

'Perhaps he thinks we know people who'd make a big fuss about the hedge,' I said. 'You know, get his name in the paper for killing wildlife and all that.'

'He deserves it,' she said frowning. 'Shall we write to the papers?'

'How can we?' I said. 'Our hide is a secret. If we tell the whole world about the hedge, they'll find out about the hide. Then there wouldn't be any point in having a hide, would there?'

'Except it might save the wildlife,' she said.

I shook my head. 'It'd ruin everything,' I told her.

'What are we going to do, then?'

'I don't know,' I said. 'I just don't know.'

It was quite late when we got home. Martin's car was parked outside the house. Holly gave a squeal of excitement and went running inside, but I took my time taking off my boots. I wasn't in a hurry to see Martin.

My mother came out to find me. 'Jake, where have you been?' she asked. 'Martin's been here for two hours. He's been longing to see Holly!'

I couldn't understand it. She had never asked me before where I'd been. It was probably Martin that had wanted to know. He was changing that too.

'We even went along to Mrs Jones's,' she went on. 'She hadn't seen you. I thought you said you'd go and see her!'

Mum looked hurt. That made me very unhappy. I wanted things to be all right between us again, but somehow I didn't know what to say. I went upstairs to be by myself.

I sat on my bed and talked to God. 'Everything's going wrong,' I said. 'I asked you to get rid of Martin and you haven't. I did try not to be nasty to him, but that didn't work. I can't stand it if he tries to check up where I go all the time. You'll have to do something, God. And please save the hedge. Please help me.'

It was a complaining prayer. I couldn't think of anything except bad things. I forgot, though, that there were good things happening. I didn't think to thank God for them. Perhaps I didn't even realise it then, but I'd changed my attitude to Holly completely. That afternoon, I'd even told Mr Grainger that she was going to be my sister!

We all ate our tea together. Martin was cold and angry and I was moody. We'd had a row – at least, Martin had told me off for taking Holly out without saying where I was going and for staying out so long, while I refused to speak. My mother was tense and anxious.

If it hadn't been for Holly, it would have been a silent meal. However, she wanted to tell her dad everything that had happened while he'd been away. She didn't say one word about the hide. She didn't even hint or wink at me or giggle when she was actually telling her dad something we'd seen from the hide. I couldn't help admiring her. Not many people of her age could have kept a secret that well.

Gradually, Martin, getting interested in what she was saying, began to thaw and relax. 'You've had such a good time,' he said, 'you must be sorry now that I've come back so early. Don't you wish you could stay the whole week?'

Holly pulled one of her funny faces. She was wondering how to answer that without upsetting either her dad or my mum.

'Well,' she said, 'I liked being here very much, but it will be even better when we're all one family and you can be here too.'

Everyone, except me, laughed at her clever answer. My mother began to look happier. The horrible atmosphere was gone.

How I envied Holly! She'd done it without realising what she was doing. Life was so easy for her. She was actually looking forward to the very thing I was dreading! I suppose it was because she got on so well with my mother. She couldn't remember her own mother. There was no one to compare Mum with. I was always comparing Martin with my dad, what I could remember of him.

I was the odd one out. I was awkward. But how could I get across my feelings to anyone? Who would listen to me?

In the next few weeks, I spilt out my thoughts to God. I always felt he was listening, though I couldn't understand why he wasn't doing what I asked.

If I hadn't learnt to talk to God, I think I'd have exploded much more often than I did. Then, I'd have hurt my mother. I'd have hated that.

Chapter six

The wedding was only a couple of days away. It was June. In the hedge, the blackbirds' nest was still there, but no blackbirds. They'd all left weeks before. As the baby birds had grown in the nest, we'd often had the chance to see them.

One day, some weeks earlier, I'd been looking across the field, trying to identify some butterflies that were dancing up and down in the warm air, when Holly had give me a gentle nudge. She'd often been with me. The hide seemed empty now when I was alone. I had followed her gaze and had seen the drab brown female sitting near the nest, thin worms dangling from her beak. She had come very close to us. I'd even seen the speckles on her chest quite clearly. Her black eyes had stared at us accusingly, but we hadn't moved. We had almost stopped breathing. She must have decided that we weren't dangerous because she had hopped from perch to perch along the hedge until she stood among the leafy branches above the nest. At once four beaks had gaped open as the baby birds rose up hopefully, and she had placed the worms carefully into each huge mouth. As soon as she'd gone, the beaks had closed and the birds had shrunk away out of our sight. This had happened several times. It had been rather like watching a machine working! It was the way the beaks opened and rose automatically as the parents arrived, then disappeared again together.

Now the fledglings had flown. We'd hoped to see them leave the nest, but they'd disappeared late one evening or early the next morning. I'd been there until almost dusk and just after breakfast the next day, but in that time the fledglings had learnt to fly. The nest was empty.

Now that there was no danger to the birds, I pushed my way through the branches to take a closer look at the nest. I put my hand inside. It was amazingly clean and very soft. The lining was made of very fine grass.

There were plenty of other things to write about in the notebook. Our latest entries were about the butterflies we'd seen. We weren't very good at identifying them because, although we had a book to help us, we found it hard to have a really good look at the patterns and colours of their wings from inside the hide.

All the time, though, we were worrying about the hide. We didn't know how much longer the hedge would stay there. Holly wanted me to do something to save it, but all her suggestions would have meant letting everyone know about it. I wanted it to remain a secret. However, I was there as much as possible. I meant to be there when Mr Grainger came with his machines!

At home, everything reminded me that Mum

was going to get married soon. Already, Martin had started moving in some of his furniture from the little cottage he shared with Holly. My dad's things, his book, his pipe stand, the photographs he'd taken, began to disappear or to take second place to Martin's belongings. It was my mother who moved things, not Martin. Perhaps she thought I hadn't noticed.

We'd had a few talks, Martin and I. He kept saying that I should try and see how my mother felt about the way I behaved.

'Don't you want her to be happy?' he'd ask.

Well, of course I did, but mostly I wanted to be happy myself – and how could I when Mum was pushing me out? Once, I told Martin that. What do you think he replied? He said, 'No one is pushing you out, Jake. You are wanted and loved as much as ever. Love isn't like a bag of sweets, you know. You can keep sharing out love – and it never gets less.'

I thought about that a lot. I could understand what he meant, but it didn't really help me with how I felt. It wasn't good enough to be told that I wasn't being pushed out. It felt as though I was – and I hated it.

Part of the trouble was that I was hardly ever on my own with Mum. She was busy planning the wedding and I was spending all the time I could in the hide. Martin was around a lot too – and Holly, of course, but that was different. I never thought of her as someone who was getting between me and my mother.

I kept all my thoughts to myself. I was often accused of being moody or unhelpful, but I was never able to explain to anyone what was going on inside my head.

Sometimes, I'd go back to those words from the Bible about 'serving each other'. If you remember, I'd thought at first that it would be all right to 'serve' by keeping myself to myself and not making anyone unhappy. Well, now I could see that it wasn't working. You see, I was keeping myself to myself – and it was upsetting everyone!

I realised that I would have to do something positive if I wanted to 'serve' those around me, but my own feelings were so huge to me that I was helpless to do anything for anyone else.

To be truthful, I honestly thought that I was the only person who needed help. I didn't see how anxious Mum was about me. I couldn't see how hard Martin was trying not to hurt my feelings. It didn't occur to me that Holly might be worrying about anything. In all my prayers, I never once asked God to change me. I thought other people needed changing, not me.

My grandmother was arriving two days before the wedding. I suppose I'd been secretly hoping that it would all be called off at the last moment, but once I knew that Grandmother was on her way, I gave up hope. Once she was with us, the wedding would certainly go ahead!

Holly and I were staring out of the front window. We'd been told to look out for Grandmother's car. As soon as we saw it pull up, one of us was to run next door and get Mum who was talking to our neighbour about flowers or something.

'I wish it was all over,' sighed Holly. Even she was fed up with everyone telling us how happy we must be, of being measured for this or that, of being told where to stand during the wedding, what to do, when to smile and so on.

'So do I,' I replied. It struck me suddenly that all the preparations that had been happening were actually going to lead to a wedding. That sounds silly, but it's one thing being told about what's going to happen, it's another to really believe you're going to have to go through with it. I began to panic!

'I'm going out!' I told Holly.

'You can't!' she cried. 'Your gran will be here soon.'

'I've got to,' I said. 'I've got to think.'

She leapt up and held onto my arm. 'Well, if you must think, think here,' she urged. 'You'll get into trouble if you're not here when she arrives.'

I pulled away from her. 'I don't care! I can't think in this house. Anyway, no one'll miss me. I won't be long.'

I was climbing the mountain again. I went fast, forcing myself on, though my legs and chest felt as though they were on fire.

'I'll never be happy again,' I thought. 'I'll have to share Mum with Martin. I'll never see her on my own.'

I had said that I wouldn't be out long, but I'd climbed almost as high as before when my legs gave out. I flopped to the ground. I was so miserable that I cried.

Then I lay still, feeling the awful loneliness of being one solitary person on the vast, empty side of the bare mountain, listening to the vacant stillness.

A buzzard soared overhead, his wings spread wide, hardly moving. Perhaps it was looking for prey, a small mammal or bird. I wondered if he had a young buzzard to feed; whether he was watching me as I was watching him. Was he summing me up as a possible meal?

I wasn't afraid. I was glad of his companionship. High above me, with his wings outstretched, he seemed of a similar size to me. I was no longer alone. He wheeled above me for a while as I lay trying to memorise the pattern of his brown feathers, black tipped wings and fan shaped tail. Then, he was gone, soaring away, gathering height.

I got to my feet and followed the bird uphill, but he was out of sight before I'd taken twenty heavy steps. Yet still I went on.

Above the grassy slopes, the mountain is just rock, mounds of granite. I had to find each foothold. There were no paths or tracks. And the higher I climbed, the more difficult it was. Some of the rock was loose. I had to test every step before I trusted my weight anywhere. Any false move sent slithers of rock slipping downwards.

Then it began to rain, just a little, enough to make the going slippery. Once my feet lost their hold. I fell hard onto the ground. Loose flakes of rock were falling all around me and I was slithering down, desperately searching for a way of stopping my fall. I stopped with a bump and lay still, my heart racing, with closed eyes, until the shower of stones and dust had stopped. Then I looked up and saw that I'd slid down a short scree. I must have missed my footing as I tried to cross it.

I was scared. I was hurt, one elbow and shoulder scraped, my head bumped, but it could have been much worse. Supposing I'd broken my leg, what would have happened to me?

I looked up. I couldn't see the summit. It was hidden from me by the slope I'd been trying to climb. I thought, 'It's defeated me this time, but I will climb it one day. Nothing is going to stop me.'

Then I began to find the way down. The trouble was that I couldn't see which way to go. It would have been easier if I'd been able to return the way I'd come, but I couldn't climb back up the scree. From where I stood I didn't even know if there was a safe way down. All I could do was to go carefully and hope I'd find an easy descent.

I kept our village in view as much as possible, though, with the cloud closing in, this was hard at times. Also, if you've ever climbed a mountain, you'll realise how difficult it is to go exactly in the direction you want to. I kept coming to walls of sheer rock, quite impossible to get down. I'd have to go back and find another route and gradually I was forced to go further and further from the way I wanted.

It was nearly dark by the time I got down to the road. This made me realise how long I'd been away from home. In June it doesn't get dark until after ten o'clock. I began to run, but I was tired and hungry. I kept stumbling. It was a long way too. I was on the right road, the one which leads into the village, but I was three or four miles away. It was a nightmare. I seemed to walk, then run, then stumble, pick myself up and walk on for hours. By the time I could see the lights shining in the front of my house, it was quite dark. I was wet through. The rain had become heavy, the drenching rain we often get in our part of the country. So, miserable, cold, wet and tired I arrived home and crept round to the back of the house. I dreaded to think what I'd have to face inside.

I squelched into the back porch, took off my boots and left them draining onto the floor. Just inside the kitchen I hung up my wet jacket and took off my damp socks. I tiptoed up the passage from the kitchen to the foot of the stairs, hoping that no one would hear me. Then, at least, I could have got into dry clothes before seeing anyone.

I was just passing the door of the front living room when it opened. Out came Martin, dressed to go out into the rain. He must have been out before. His orange anorak and trousers were wet already. Behind him, in the room, were my mother and my grandmother and Holly, who was ready for bed. There was a moment, which seemed to go on for ages, when no one spoke. I don't know which was worse – that moment or everything which followed.

Early next morning, there was a soft knock at my door and Holly came in.

'Why aren't you at home?' I asked.

'Well, I was going to sleep here because Daddy was out looking for you. Sue put up a camp bed for me. So, when you turned up, she said I'd better sleep here anyway because I was ready for bed.' She padded over and sat on my bed. 'What happened last night?' she asked. 'I didn't hear much shouting.'

'There wasn't any,' I told her. 'Just people talking on and on about how disappointed in me they were, and how I ought to be looking after Mum now, not giving her frights.'

'Did my dad say that?'

I nodded. 'So did my grandmother. They went on and on and on.'

'What did Sue say?' she asked. 'She was really scared. She thought you'd been killed!'

I thought that over. 'She didn't say a word, just looked at me. It was worse really. Martin told me off most.'

'He was worried too,' Holly told me. 'He kept going out, looking for you and coming back in case you'd turned up.'

I scowled. 'He was mad at me! I hated him!'

She screwed up her face. 'Don't,' she pleaded. 'Don't hate him. Last night, when he was tired, his face was all tight and worried. He went out in the rain for hours, just to look for you. How can you hate him?'

There were tears in her eyes. 'I think I know why you ran off, Jake. I get funny feelings too when I think of living with you and Sue all the time. Oh please don't go and make things horrible, Jake. Please be nice to Dad. You used to be horrible to me and now you're nice, so I know you can change.'

I said, 'I started being nice to you because you were nice to me.'

'No, Jake, you started it. Don't you remember? I was horrible to you because I was scared of you. Then you changed. You showed me the hide and we were friends.'

She was right.

As soon as I was alone I talked to God again. I prayed, 'Lord Jesus, you changed me and helped me be nice to Holly. I'm sorry I've been so selfish. I've upset everyone, even Mum. I've done everything wrong and made it hard for her and for Martin. Please forgive me and help me be nice to Martin.'

It was something like that, anyway. It's hard to remember exactly what I prayed, but afterwards I felt better than I had for weeks. I was going to try and make our new family happy!

Chapter seven

It was the day before the wedding. My grandmother was in charge in the kitchen, cooking meals and getting drinks and snacks nearly the whole day. I was kept busy most of the time looking after relations who were arriving from all over the country.

To tell the truth, I was quite glad when, after tea, things went quiet for a while and I was able to slip away to be by myself.

I went to the hide. The ground was still sticky after the heavy rain and I knew that I mustn't go back to the house muddy. Grandmother has never been as understanding about that sort of things as my mother. So I just went to the field and squatted down by the hedge, hiding in the bracken as much as I could.

After the noise and bustle of the house that day, I loved the quietness and stillness. I'd been so busy with other people, I hadn't had any time to think properly since Holly had come to my bedroom.

She had made me realise how the others were feeling and made me ashamed of being so self-centred. That prayer had come straight from my heart, but now I could see that it wasn't going to be easy working to make a happy family.

'What,' I thought, 'if I do so much to help others and, all the time, I'm miserable myself? I can't see how I'm ever going to like having Martin around the whole time.'

True enough, when I'd started to be nice to Holly, it had worked well. I'd got happier myself. Even sharing the hide had become a pleasure. Would it work the same if I started to be nice to Martin, or would I end up even more miserable?

As I was turning this over in my mind, my eyes picked out a bird flying across the field. By the way it flicked up its tail as it landed I spotted, though it was still distant, that it was a blackbird. It ran a little, then stopped, head up cautiously. After a few seconds it flapped into flight and landed not far from me. It was a female, perhaps even *my* female blackbird. As she stood there near the hedge, her head cocked, I saw that she had some strands of grass in her beak. Motionless for a moment, she looked about, then dipped her head and seemed to wipe her beak in the mud. At the same time, I spotted her mate, who flew in beside her and watched as she flew into the hedge.

I couldn't see where she went, but I was excited. The blackbirds had returned to build another nest! Perhaps this time I'd see the fledglings leave the nest! If only she was making it closer to the hide, we'd have an even better view than before.

But I daren't go in, not only because I didn't want to get muddy, but for fear of disturbing them. I stayed where I was until my legs were so cramped that I had to move. By that time both the birds had gone backwards and forwards with grass and twigs several times. While they were both away I stood up slowly and carefully eased myself out of the bracken.

'What a shame!' I thought. 'I've got a piece of really exciting news and I can't tell Holly.'

Several times that night I was told, by all my relations, including my grown up cousins, how to behave the next day.

'Stand up straight, Jake, keep as tidy as you can and smile!'

I got tired of it, especially when they added, as some did, 'Aren't you thrilled to be having a new father?'

I was sure I was going to get everything wrong the next day and not a bit happy about people calling Martin my new father, so I got more and more tense as time went by.

In the morning, my grandmother got me up early and had me helping in the kitchen. She thrust a tray of food into my hands and said, 'Take this up to your mother, Jake, and hurry down. Your breakfast will be ready in a minute.'

'Grandmother says I've got to hurry,' I told Mum as I dumped the tray into her lap. She was sitting up in bed already, but still looking sleepy.

'She'll have to wait,' my mother said. 'Come and sit beside me, Jake. Things'll get hectic later, but I want to see you before I start on all that.' She pushed the tray to one side to make room for me.

So I sat close to her and she put her arm around me. I was pleased. Recently, we'd been like strangers living in the same house, hardly talking except about day to day things like what was for supper and where my clean socks were. I don't suppose I'd made it easy for my mother to show me much affection. I'd been very grumpy.

'This won't happen again,' I said sadly. 'Martin will be here.'

'It certainly will happen,' she said. 'Don't you think Martin knows that I want to be alone with you sometimes?'

'I don't know,' I told her.

'Of course he does. We've been thinking about it a lot. And don't forget that I won't be working in the afternoons any more. That'll mean a lot more time together. You might even begin to wish that I wasn't here so much.'

'That'll never happen,' I said.

She laughed. 'Wait and see, Jake. We will be happy, I promise.'

I told her, 'I want us to be, but I do feel scared.'

'We all do,' she said, 'but part of our wedding service will be a prayer that Jesus will be part of our family. We needn't be scared if he is with us, need we? He's the one who'll keep us together, you know. When we ask him into our lives and say that he is our Lord, we mean that we'll learn to live in the way he wants. You have done that, haven't you?'

I nodded. I'd been brought up to believe that you should do what God wants, not just what you want. I also knew that I was beginning to follow Jesus for myself. I've told you about some of the changes in my life. Jesus was always obedient to his Father God and I was learning to be like him, not very fast, but I'd begun!

'Then don't be scared,' Mum said. 'You and me, Martin and Holly, we'll all be trying to help each other, not just trying to get the best for ourselves. Do you agree?'

I couldn't tell her all that had helped me understand what she'd said. The words wouldn't come to my mouth, but I nodded again so that she'd know what I thought. I heard my grandmother calling me, but Mum held on to me.

'Thank you, Jake, I knew you'd understand. And if things do go wrong at any time, promise me you'll come and talk to me. Promise me you'll be honest with me always.'

Again I nodded and slid off the bed. 'I'd better go.' I said. I was about to open the door when I changed my mind and went back. 'I haven't been honest,' I admitted.

'I know, Jake. It's been hard for you to talk about how you feel about me getting married – '

I hung my head. 'No, not that. I broke a promise – ' And, in a rush, I began to confess how I'd gone onto the mountain, not once, but twice and how sorry I was. It had been like a mountain itself, this broken promise, standing between me and Mum, but as I blurted it out, the mountain began to crumble and fall away. I felt Mum's hand gripping mine.

'Oh Jake,' she whispered when I'd finished, 'please don't ever do that again.' I looked up and saw that she'd forgiven me, but I felt how sad she was with me. 'Promise you won't,' she went on. 'I just couldn't bear to lose you.'

I went downstairs feeling happy that I'd put things right with my mother, but at the same time I remembered her sadness. So it was a serious happiness, not the type that makes you want to leap about.

My grandmother was cross, though not with me. 'What does Sue think she's doing keeping you so long?' she cried. 'Doesn't she realise how much I've got to get done? Your breakfast's cold, I'm afraid, but it's not my fault. Eat it quickly and then go and knock up your Aunt Lucy and Uncle David. They promised they'd be down early to help.'

I smiled secretly. Poor Gran! My mother and Aunt Lucy were both her daughters and neither of them liked getting up in the morning!

The funny thing was that despite my grandmother's fuss, the work was finished in no time. She's a good organiser, my grandmother, not like my mother!

Far too early, I thought, she sent me to change. I washed again – she'd said I had to – brushed my hair (again) and dressed in the new grey suit that had taken so much measuring and fitting. I looked in the mirror and thought I looked pretty silly. I never wear a suit normally. I hoped that Holly wouldn't laugh when she saw me later.

Then I heard a noise. It sounded like a tractor engine. I put my head out of the window, but I couldn't see anything. My room is at the front of the house. The noise was coming from the field at the back. I began to worry. Was it today, of all days, that Mr Grainger was going to grub out the hedge?

There was no time to waste. I had to get to the field, but I must get there without being seen by anyone else. They would not let me go if they caught me. So I found my new shiny shoes and slipped them on. I raced down the stairs and out of the front door. 'So far, so good,' I thought.

The tricky part was getting by all the windows on the side of the house. I didn't look in, but I guess someone must have seen me. I pretended I was going for a stroll in the garden in case anyone was looking. I took a chance by running all the way down the back garden. There was no other way of getting into the field quickly enough. All the time, the throb of the tractor made my heart bump uncomfortably. I had to know what was going on.

The tractor was standing, engine still running, in the further part of the field, so I dived through the hedge where it was thinnest and ran across to Mr Grainger who was sitting in the cab.

'Hey!' I called, but he didn't hear me.

'Hey' I yelled running closer. That time he heard and climbed out onto the ground.

'You're not going to pull out that hedge!' I panted.

He looked startled and I had to repeat what I'd said before he could understand me.

'I've told you once, young Collier,' he said.

'Not today?' I pleaded.

The farmer shook his head. 'But I will in a week or two perhaps, and it's no good trying to talk me out of it.'

'Please don't,' I begged. 'Look, there's blackbirds nesting in there right now and several sorts of mammals living there. My sister's counted ten different kinds of insects in the leaf litter and eight different kinds of – ' I had an idea. 'Look, I'll get something,' I interrupted myself.

'I haven't got time to waste on – ' Mr Grainger began.

Quickly I replied, 'No, it's just here. I won't be a second.' While I was talking I was running to the hedge. I crashed in. A bird rose out of the hedge chattering loudly and flapping away angrily. It must have been a blackbird disturbed from the nest, but I didn't care. I was in a hurry. I dug out our notebook, leaving on one side the stone under which we used to hide it. Crawling out of the hide, I pulled off the plastic cover that protected it.

I thrust it under Mr Grainger's nose and turned the pages, talking very fast, telling him all that we'd observed in the last few weeks. I jabbed my finger at entry after entry, hoping to make him see how important the hedge was.

At last, he pushed it aside. 'This is all very well, young Collier, but I'm talking about money. When I want to move my sheep from here to there,' he said, pointing to the other side of the hedge, 'I've got to get my dogs, and take them up the road and down the other side. If it was all one field, there'd be no need for all that bother. My time's money to me, you know.'

'Can't you see what the hedge means,' I shouted, much too loudly. 'It's the wildlife. There's nowhere else like this round here. Why do you have to take it *all* out?'

He glared at me. 'I've told you – money and time. And you're wasting them now. Off my land, and I don't want to hear any more from you!'

My head was so full of the argument that I didn't realise, until I reached the back door, what a mess I was in. My new suit was not only torn but smeared with wet mud. My shoes were clogged with it. I was horrified. What ever was I going to do?

I opened the door a very little and listened. It was quiet in the kitchen so I crept inside.

Nobody was there. The dining room beyond was empty too and so was the passage that leads to the stairs. From the front living room came a murmur of voices, the tinkling of spoons and cups and the aroma of coffee. Excellent, now I really had a chance of getting to my room without being seen!

Just when I really thought I'd made it, my hand on the doorknob of my room, another door opened and someone came out. It was my mother.

I don't really remember much about what people were wearing, but I know, from looking at the photographs taken later, that she was wearing a blue dress and jacket. I do remember that I thought she looked lovely, her hair all tidy for a change. And I felt terrible.

She took one look at me and her eyes grew so large I couldn't believe it! 'Oh Jake,' she cried, not too loudly. Then, 'Quick! Into my room. Shut the door and don't let anyone in but me.'

My grandmother said I looked 'very smart' as she pinned a flower onto my shirt. But later I did hear Aunt Lucy say to her, 'What a pity that Sue didn't get him a proper suit for such a special day!'

I hoped that no one had seen the muddy splashes in the bathroom. We'd had to wash my shoes under the tap. They were damp inside all day. The grey suit was hidden in Mum's wardrobe so that no one would ever know what had happened.

When I think of how she dealt with it, I'm proud of my mum. She could have ruined the day for me by telling everyone what I'd done. She didn't let on to a soul. It's our secret.

Chapter eight

The wedding was over! I don't suppose you want to know much about it. The best part, I promise, was the food afterwards – a real feast! We could help ourselves to as much as we could eat. Nobody spoilt it by telling us not to be greedy, not even my grandmother, though she did look horrified when she saw me and Holly going up for our fifth helpings.

She couldn't have minded, though, because afterwards when we were alone at home, she sighed, 'What a lovely wedding! And weren't you a good boy, Jake?'

I hate people saying things like that, but I didn't mind that day. She'd have said far worse than that if she'd known how I'd ruined my new suit earlier!

'Holly was a sweet bridesmaid,' she went on. 'And Martin is such a good sort of man. I'm glad to see Sue settled again with such a nice family.'

She was right. We were a family now. Nothing could change that. I'd never live alone with my mother again. People make important promises to God when they get married. They say that they will love each other and stick together no matter what. They ask God to help them keep their promises. I knew that Mum and Martin meant to keep theirs.

It seemed very quiet in the house – just my grandmother and me. All the guests had gone. Holly was staying with an aunt of hers. Mum and Martin had gone away for a few days.

Grandmother was tired and dropped off to sleep in her chair. I went to change my clothes, put the notebook from the hide into my pocket (I'd brought it back into the house after showing it to Mr Grainger that morning) and went outside.

I walked slowly down the garden, enjoying the early evening sunshine. Since I'd known Holly properly, our back garden had become much more interesting to me. The plants I'd thought were 'just weeds' were wild flowers to her. She taught me to look at them.

There were yellow clusters of flowers that were attracting several kinds of insects. I'd just thought of them as funny dandelions, but Holly told me they were nippleworts.

'And did you know,' she'd said, 'the name "dandelion" means "lion's tooth" in French, because the leaves are shaped like huge teeth.'

Growing everywhere was chickweed, which flowers all year round. My mother complains about how it spreads, but Holly made me look at it. 'Its proper name,' she had told me, 'means "little star". Look at the tiny white flowers. They're just like five pointed stars, aren't they?'

After squeezing through the gap in the fence, I wandered about in the field, looking for more of the flowers that Holly had shown me. Wherever I walked flies and butterflies and other insects flew up in front of me, then resettled on the flowers.

Some of these flowers attracted my attention quickly. The field stands high with cow parsley spreading out its large white heads. Others need looking for. There were patches of red clover, which, Holly said, attract insects with their scent, though only those with long tongues can feed from them, because the nectar is deep inside the petals. I found some borage, a herb with hairy leaves, and also comfrey. Neither of these plants are pretty, mostly the flowers are half hidden in the large leaves, but they were both used as medicines in the old days. The insects seemed to know they were good. I found bees busy at the flowers.

Close to the hedge were some delicate violets, very pale with heart-shaped leaves. I wandered over to see them, got out the notebook and began to draw them. How I wished I could draw like Holly! I would have liked to have made them look as they really were, nodding in the gentle breeze.

It was a hot evening despite the breeze which dislodged tiny white parachutes from the sorrel, sending the seeds floating across the field. The ground had almost dried and I was able to sit by the hedge without getting too wet. I watched swallows and martins skimming across in front of me, catching insects on the wing. I saw a thrush cracking open a snail's shell on a rock. A couple of whitethroats were darting in and out of the hedge. A pair of crows seemed to be wasting time walking backwards and forwards where the grass was sparse. Yet I saw no blackbirds.

I waited for an hour or more, sitting by the hedge, almost hidden, but there was no flash of shiny black feathers, no yellow bill, nor the brown female blending into the background. Where could they be? Surely with a new nest they ought to be about – unless they were already in the hedge and not moving at present.

Cautiously I found my usual entrance to the hide and crept inside. I looked about, hoping to see the new nest, but there was nothing, only the old one. There was no bird near it.

I eased forward, pushing my way between the branches until I was close to the nest. Carefully, I straightened up as much as I could and peered over the edge. The nest contained four tiny eggs, greenish blue with brown speckles. So, the birds had simply repaired the old nest, not made another!

I pushed my arm up, careful not to snap any twigs, and touched the grassy inside. How do birds make nests so well just using a beak? With one finger I reached further and touched one egg. It was cold!

'Oh no!' I cried out. I froze, my hand in mid air. Then, afraid, I touched another egg, then the others in turn. They were all as cold as stone. They should have been warmer than my hand, even if the parents had left them for a short while. They would certainly have returned before the eggs got this cold – unless – unless (this was an uncomfortable thought) unless they'd been frightened off.

That morning I had stormed into the hedge

to get the notebook to show Mr Grainger. My thoughtlessness had scared the birds away. They'd abandoned the nest!

I crawled back to the hide where the upturned stone accused me. I sat for a long time, until the air was full of the night song of birds and the light was fading, willing the blackbirds to come back. Of course, they didn't and if they had it would have been too late. The eggs were cold. There would be no chicks. And it was my fault.

I'd told Holly and I'd told Mr Grainger that we had to save the hedge because of the wildlife. I could see now that it hadn't been the true reason. Of course I did care about the birds and animals and the flowers, but what I had cared about most was myself. If I'd truly wanted not to harm the wildlife, I'd never have gone rushing carelessly into the hide. I'd have remembered the blackbirds and stayed away.

I walked home, deeply unhappy with myself. I was so selfish. It was always the same. How could I change?

Even my grandmother agreed that I was well behaved during those few days until Mum came home – yes, even Grandmother who usually clicks her tongue and shakes her head over the things I get up to. But I was unhappy inside. Being on your best behaviour all the time is very uncomfortable. So is feeling guilty.

I wished things could get back to normal, but they never would. Mum was coming home soon, but Martin would come too. And I'd have to face Holly and tell her what had happened in the hide. And I'd have to go on being on my best behaviour because I'd promised to make our family happy together. Not much to look forward to, I thought.

There were a few surprises coming, though! When Mum and Martin came home with Holly, they all had presents for me. It wasn't even my birthday!

Holly's present was a hat. She'd been knitting at her aunt's. It had been meant for herself, but she'd made it too big. 'Keep it for winter,' she said.

Mum gave me something funny. It was a plaster figure to put on my bedroom shelf. I couldn't think why she'd bought it. I'd never had anything like it before.

'Take a proper look at it,' she said with a laughing smile.

Then I understood. It was a boy dressed in a brown suit and tie, but it was the most ragged suit I've ever seen, and the tie was all twisted around. His feet were poking out of his shoes. I blushed and smiled at her, hoping she wasn't going to tell the others why she'd given it to me. I understood the joke, but I didn't want to share it.

As for Martin's present, it was magnificent – a pair of binoculars, not new, but in perfect condition. It was what I'd always wanted. I didn't know how to say 'thank you' properly.

Holly had presents too. She hugged both Martin and my mother. 'I'm so pleased,' she said. 'Thank you very much.' Then she hugged them again. I just stood there, holding my presents, feeling silly and awkward. All I managed to say was, 'Thanks'.

I felt awkward all the time for a few days. There was so much to get used to. Martin and Holly were there all the time – in the evening and early in the morning. We had to do things in new ways, but I'll say more about that later. First, I'd better tell you the good things that happened. Otherwise, you'll think we were miserable together.

Well, we weren't, not even me. I had to admit that life was more fun! The best thing of all was that my mother suddenly seemed to have more energy. She smiled a lot and got things done a lot quicker. I suppose she hadn't got so many worries and had more time, not being out at work all day. She looked very happy.

We laughed a lot. Everything seemed so funny to us in those first few days together. We still often enjoy a joke, but not half as often as we did then. Perhaps it was because we were trying so hard not to upset each other. You see, when you think about it, it's ridiculous to spend half an hour discussing something like where to keep the teapot!

But that's the sort of thing that used to happen. Then Holly would get the giggles and we'd all end up laughing!

It's funny, you take things for granted, like what brand of toothpaste you use, where you clean shoes, what sort of rubbish goes in which bin – until someone comes along with different ideas. Then you have to change everything.

I'll say this for Martin, though, he never complained about the way Mum did things. He had lots of suggestions for doing things more tidily or more quickly, but he never moaned when something wasn't done in the way he thought best.

He moaned at me, though. And that's really what started things going wrong.

As far as I could see, there were two sides to having Martin around.

The good side was that hardly a week passed without us going out somewhere interesting. Like Holly, Martin loves being in the countryside. We did a lot of walking together. I soon found out just how Holly knows so much about nature. As we walked, Martin was forever pointing out what caught his eye, things that I would have missed on my own. He even knows the names of grasses!

'Look,' he might say kneeling down, 'did you know this grass is called "sheep's fescue"? It grows well up here on the mountain pasture. See the violet tinge to the spiky flowers?'

Holly would take a piece and keep it carefully until we got home. Then she'd draw it. And I'd spend some time examining it so that I'd always recognise the grass again.

I took my binoculars on our walks, but Martin's eyes were quicker than mine, even with the binoculars.

'A marsh harrier!' he'd cry, pointing at the sky.

Often by the time I'd located the shape in the sky, it was a blur in the distance, high above the horizon. Yet Martin had seen it and told me how to recognise this bird of prey which visits our mountain in the summer – long straight tail, wings and body, long legs, the bird flying head down, wings angled upwards.

Sometimes I was glad to be learning so much from him. I could see that my mother was pleased that Martin and I had this interest in common. She liked the trips out too. We always enjoyed ourselves, but sometimes I felt angry – because I wanted my own dad to tell me all these things, not Martin. Of course, that was impossible, so I never let on how I felt. I didn't think anyone would understand.

The other side of having Martin living with us was that he began to criticise me. And my mother let him!

Quite often, in the old days at weekends, I hadn't got dressed until late in the morning. I used to get up when I wanted to and then help myself to breakfast before getting dressed. The first time I did this after the wedding, Martin said, 'I think it would be better if you got up earlier, Jake. I'd rather you had breakfast with us. Will you please get dressed before you come down, too?'

I looked at my mother to see if she'd say anything. She asked, 'Does it really matter, Martin?'

'It does to me,' he said. 'I don't want Jake to think it's all right to drift around, wasting his time.'

I said, 'I don't care. It's only Saturday. There's nothing much to do.'

'You should care,' he replied. 'There's plenty to do. Time should be used wisely, not wasted.'

We had a long argument about that, but I lost. My mother said nothing the whole time. All she said afterwards to me was, 'It's not such a big change to make, is it, Jake?'

I also lost the argument about watching television. Martin started that one when he found me watching a film late one night. He said it wasn't suitable for me, and I ought to be in bed anyway. My mother even agreed with him, though I'd been allowed to watch that sort of film before.

There were lots of jobs for both Holly and me too. Holly was used to it, but I wasn't. It seemed hard to me, having to do chores every day, not just when I wanted to.

One way and another, I began to feel that Martin was having everything far too much his own way, but, for a while, I just put up with it.

We went on praying together. Martin was quite strict about it. I know it would have been forgotten lots of times if it had been up to me or my mother! Praying was soon part of my life, a normal daily thing to do. And I began to tell God that, on the whole, things weren't as bad as I'd thought they'd be.

'But please,' I'd say in secret, 'don't let Martin get too bossy.'

Chapter nine

'You killed them!' wailed Holly. 'Poor little birds! How could you, Jake?'

We were standing at the end of the garden near to the place that Martin had tried to dig over to make a vegetable patch. It was so full of stones, however, that he had given up.

Neither Holly nor I had been to the hide for weeks. She'd suggested it several times, but I'd always put her off. Sometimes I'd taken her somewhere else instead, and at other times I'd given her an excuse. She couldn't go on her own any more because Martin didn't like her out of the house alone for long.

That day, she'd tried to insist. In the end, I'd given in, but before going, just in case she saw the blackbirds' eggs, I had to explain about how the nest had been abandoned.

'It was an accident,' I explained. 'I didn't mean to frighten the birds. I had to show Mr Grainger the notebook to make him understand. I just reached in.'

'You killed them!' she shouted. 'You don't really care, do you?'

That made me mad. 'Yes, I do! I keep telling you – it was an accident!'

Holly was pulling one of her meanest faces. 'I'll never speak to you again!' she yelled. 'I wanted to see those baby birds.'

'They were only eggs!' I scoffed. 'You didn't even know about them until today.'

She glared at me. 'That doesn't make any difference. I still wanted to see them. I'm going to see the eggs anyway. Don't try and stop me.' She ran a little way, then turned back. 'Don't follow me!' she yelled.

Sadly, I went back indoors. I was sorry she'd taken it so badly. We hadn't got on quite so well since the wedding. I was upset about that too.

It was a Saturday. Upstairs Martin and Mum were starting to decorate Holly's bedroom. I heard them shifting furniture as I went up the stairs. They were making so much noise that they didn't hear me.

When they began to speak, I stopped still, listening. I thought I'd like to know how they talked when they were alone. It was a horrible thing to do, I know, but that didn't stop me.

They were obviously finishing off something they'd been talking about before. I realised quickly that it was about me. Then I wished that I wasn't listening.

'Just try to remember that he's not used to having a man about,' my mother was saying. 'I know I've been a bit lax with him. It's not always easy to cope with him. He's very strong-willed – and I'm not. But please don't be too hard on him all at once.'

Then Martin said, 'I don't mean to be, Sue. The last thing I want to do is to upset you. But some things are important, aren't they? I have to make him help in the house, for instance, because I've always expected Holly to. I can't just let him off, can I? And how can I insist on knowing where Holly is always and then let Jake go off just as he likes? I know he's older, but not that much.'

'He always has done as he liked,' she said. 'I never worried where he was. He's capable of looking after himself.'

'I can't see that it's safe,' Martin said. 'Will you let me talk to him at least? I'm fond of Jake, Sue, and I worry about him, even if you don't. I can see I ought to ease up about some things, like I did about the clothes Holly wears, but I don't think this is one of them.'

I didn't hear her reply. They began to move the furniture again and I went on walking upstairs. The doorway of Holly's room was wide open. As I went by, Martin saw me and called me in. I knew just what was coming.

He made a big thing out of it, but it came down to this: in future, I had to say where I was going before I went out and say how long I'd be. 'Just in case something happened to you,' he said. 'At least I'd know where to start looking.'

'What could happen?' I asked.

'An accident – anything. I don't like you going out alone in any case.'

Mum said, 'Oh Martin, don't try to stop him! He's so careful and reliable. What could happen so long as he stays off the mountain?'

'Lots of things,' he said. He looked at her. 'We ought to know where he is, Sue.'

She looked at me. 'We ought to,' she told me. 'It's not too much to ask, is it?'

I frowned. 'I don't always know where I'm going,' I told them.

'Well,' said Martin, 'I'm not going to argue with you, Jake. You'll just have to plan ahead in future. I must know where you're going before you go out.'

Glaring at him, I replied, 'I don't see how you can make me. Besides, you don't even know where Holly is right now, do you?'

My mother gasped, 'Oh Jake, don't speak like that!'

I saw Martin open his mouth to yell at me, but stop himself. Instead, he snapped, 'What do you mean? Where is Holly?'

Angry as I was, I couldn't answer him, even if I'd wanted to. 'Wouldn't you like to know?' I jeered and I turned and ran down the stairs. Martin was after me, but he was slower than me. I had my trainers on already or he'd have caught me in the porch. I was half way down the garden before I heard the back door slam shut behind him. At the end of the garden, where you squeeze through the fence, I met Holly.

She was in tears, her face red and blotchy. She squealed when she saw me, 'He's pulling the hedge down. He's doing it now!'

I pushed her to one side. I heard Martin yell my name, but I took no notice. I knew he couldn't follow me through the fence. I heard him talking loudly to Holly, but I don't know what he said. I only listened to the thrum of the tractor. I only saw the ropes and the men swarming around my hedge, about to destroy it.

I stood in the field for only a second. I knew that there was nothing I could do. I just couldn't watch. As fast as I could, I ran across the field, over the wall and upwards – up into the mountain.

I don't really know what I was thinking as I climbed. I was just running away. I was running from what was happening to my hide. I was running from what was happening at home – running, out of breath, to the only thing I thought I had left, my dream, the mountain top.

I couldn't have kept up that furious pace for long. As the incline got steeper, I slowed. Sometimes I came to a halt in mid-stride, trying to ease my burning chest, my aching back and legs. Then I pushed myself on, head down, seeing only the ground in front of me.

When I looked up to check my direction, the jagged rocks loomed threateningly above me as though they didn't want me to go on. They couldn't stop me, nor could that blazing sun which was beating on my head and back.

I knelt to drink whenever I crossed a stream. The water was cold and pure. I splashed it on my face and let it run down my T-shirt to cool my body. Once I even took off my trainers and socks to bathe my feet. The chill as I plunged my hot, sticky feet into the water was unbearable, but wonderful. It was like blades cutting into my skin until I got used to the iciness. I sat for a while, letting the warm air blow my feet dry, then put my socks and trainers back on and climbed again.

Grimly I went on. If I was making my dream come true, I didn't feel it. I just thought of each step as a battle, followed by another. Sometimes I got lost and couldn't see which way to go. Sometimes I climbed into impossible places and had to go back on myself and try again. And there was always the danger of dislodging rocks or of slipping as I had last time I'd climbed the mountain.

Stubbornness made me go on. I was determined to reach the summit, but, even when I'd got the worst of the steep climb behind me, my problems were not over.

There is a cairn, a pile of stones, that marks the highest point of the mountain, but I couldn't find it. Near the top, one peak looks the same as several others. Having no map, I couldn't guess which was the highest. I had to search around, climbing one peak after another before I spotted the cairn in the distance.

Then, for the first time, I could see the end of my climb and set out on the last, tired walk across the bare rock.

And there I was. I had climbed the mountain. I stood in the place of my dreams.

I should have felt happy and excited. I didn't. All I felt was the ache of tired limbs and a nasty sense of guilt.

I couldn't bear to look down into my own valley. My eyes wandered idly over the view in other directions. I saw mountains far huger than the one on which I stood; other valleys, different villages and towns, lakes and streams and, in the distance, the sea. Everything was so far away. I was the only person for miles. There were no birds, no animals, hardly any plants, not even the sound of water up there, only the empty wind cooling, then chilling me.

No one knew I was there.

'Anything could happen,' Martin had said.

I saw that he was right. Supposing I had an accident and couldn't move. How would anyone find me? I had no whistle to attract attention. I could shout, but only for a while. I had no colourful clothing to make me stand out against the rock. I had no torch to signal in the darkness. I was also without food and without a way of keeping warm when the sun sank.

My mother had trusted me, though I'd let her down before. My father had been an expert climber, but he had never gone into the mountains without any preparation. I'd let him down as badly as I'd let my mother down.

And Martin and Holly? Yes, I'd let them down too. They cared about me in their different ways and now that we belonged together, the things I did affected them. I knew I would have to go home and admit what I'd done. Did I have enough courage?

I left the summit without looking back. As I began to descend, I realised just how tired I was. I'd climbed up so fast, hardly stopping, except to bathe my feet. And getting down a mountain can be even harder than going up. You have to be careful not to slip and fall headlong.

At times, I thought I just couldn't go any further. I sat down on the rocks, exhausted and hungry, and almost gave up hope. Yet each time I remembered that there was no chance for me if I stayed there. Somehow I managed to find enough strength to go a little further. The trouble was that it was so very slow.

Once I'd passed the highest stone wall and was walking where the grass and bracken grow, I felt better. From time to time, I'd see some of Mr Grainger's sheep with the red 'T' marked on their backs. They didn't take any notice of me, but I was glad to see them. At least they knew where I was!

I was still on the higher slopes, when I saw a sheep lying on its side over by one of the walls. At first, I simply stared, afraid that it was dead. I took a few steps towards it, but then I froze, full of fear.

Which would be worse, I wondered, if it was dead, or if it was alive, but injured and in terrible pain? I had to find out, despite the fact that I had to walk some distance out of my way. All I really wanted was some food and rest, but I couldn't leave a suffering animal alone on the hillside.

Every step I took seemed like a million. Alive or dead?

I watched the animal for any sign of life. Then, when I'd got within a few metres of her, she lifted her head slightly and gave a wickering bleat. Flies rose up as she moved, then settled back on her blood-caked legs.

I leapt back in fright. I had to help. Tired as I was, I must find Mr Grainger. I set off in the direction of his house. Then I remembered where he would be. Holly had heard that first conversation about the hedge. She'd told me that it would take all day to pull it out. The day was not quite over, so I guessed he'd still be there, in the field completing the destruction of my hedge.

Why should I help to save one of his animals? I never even thought that I wouldn't. I'm sure God was with me then. All selfish thoughts, of getting home as fast as I could and of paying Mr Grainger back for not saving the hedge, just melted away before I'd even considered them. All I had on my mind was the sheep and how to get help to her fast.

New strength came from nowhere. I was hurrying. I almost ran across the fields towards home. Everything else was forgotten. I was looking for Mr Grainger. Nothing else mattered.

'Hey! Hey!'

Long before I reached my field, I spotted the figure of Mr Grainger striding towards his house. He was alone, no other men, no tractor.

'Hey! Mr Grainger!' I yelled.

I ran full pelt the last hundred metres while he stoppped by a gate waiting for me.

'What's up, young Collier?' he asked while I tried to catch my breath.

I told him about the sheep. 'Up there,' I said pointing. 'She looks bad.'

He followed my directions with his eyes.

'Up there between the second and third walls,' I explained. 'She's on her side.'

He nodded. 'I'll go up,' he promised. 'I'll just go and tell the missus where I'm going. She's expecting me.'

That reminded me that I was late – and in trouble.

'I'd better go home too,' I said, 'or I'd show you where the sheep is.'

'I'll find her,' he said, opening the gate to let

me through. 'I'll take the dogs. Thanks for letting me know.'

'Goodbye,' I said and began to hurry down the track that led over the fields to home.

'By the way,' he called after me, and I stopped and turned around. 'Your hedge – ' he began. 'Have you seen it?'

'You've pulled it out,' I said dully. 'I know.'

'No,' he told me. 'It's still there. You gave me an idea, young Collier, that day. In the end, I've saved your hedge and saved myself a bit of money.'

'What do you mean?' I asked.

'Go on home,' he replied with half a smile. 'You'll see for yourself.'

I ran. My legs were as heavy as blocks of stone, but I ran. Had he saved my hide? Was everything really all right?

Soon I had the hedge in sight, but not clearly enough in the dusk to see exactly what Mr Grainger had meant. Certainly the hedge was still there!

Then I saw the scar, the patch of fresh earth and a great gap in the hedge. An ugly metal gate had been erected across the gap.

I stood and gazed in disbelief. It must be a dream – a bad dream! The hedge was safe for the wildlife, but my hide was gone. Mr Grainger, without knowing it, had taken out the very place I'd wanted so much to save.

Chapter ten

It was not quite dark when I saw a beam of light across the field. I had been sitting for some time by the gate where my hide had been. I was cold, hungry, tired and miserable, but still I couldn't go home.

I was scared. I wanted home for its warmth and comfort, but I didn't want the trouble I'd have to face there, not after the two bitter disappointments I'd had that day. In the old days, Mum would have made it easy for me. Martin wouldn't. I was certain of that.

Then I heard my own name being called, 'Jake!' The voice sounded tired as though it had been calling for a very long time. It was Martin.

'Here!' I called back. 'I'm here!'

The beam of light turned towards me. I stood up so that Martin could spot me more easily. In a minute or less, I was in his arms.

I'd expected him to shout, not to hug me. I couldn't speak. He said, still holding me, 'I've been looking for you all afternoon. Thank God you're safe.'

'I'm sorry,' I mumbled. 'I really am.'

He pushed me back a little and looked into my face. 'This mustn't happen again, Jake. You and I will have to sort things out between us. But let's go home quickly now. Sue's nearly out of her mind with worry.'

I felt ashamed.

'Holly's not much better,' he added. 'She won't stop crying.'

We walked over the field, Martin lighting up the ground in front of us. He asked, 'Jake, did you really climb up the mountain today?'

'Yes,' I admitted with shame. 'How did you know?'

'I've just seen Mr Grainger. I called at his house to see whether he'd seen you at all. He told me he'd just seen you coming down the mountain.'

'Yes, I did,' I said.

Martin sighed. 'Was it my fault, Jake?' he asked. 'I've been thinking all afternoon, looking for you. Did you run off because of me? Did I drive you into doing this stupid thing?'

'That was only part of it,' I told him.

We stopped by the fence. 'You can get through here, can't you?' he said. 'I'll have to walk around by the road.' He put his hand on my shoulder. 'What you've done today was very wrong, Jake. I think you know that, but I am sorry for my part in it. I've been pushing you too hard to change, I think, without talking things over with you properly. I won't have a chance to say that once we get home, but I want you to know I'm sorry.'

That was the moment when I really began to respect Martin. I smiled as a way of showing it and then went through the fence. I went into the house on my own. Not until then did my exhaustion hit me. I sat on the kitchen floor trying to pull off my trainers. I just couldn't do it.

I hadn't expected Martin to hug me – and I didn't expect my mum to shout at me. But she did. She was upset and angry.

She pulled off my shoes and sat me on a kitchen chair. She heated some soup for me, cut some bread and gave them to me. All the time, she shouted at me. I knew I deserved it.

'This has shown me that Martin's right,' she said. 'We have to know where you are – all the time. I've been worried to death, Jake. I rang all your friends, the police, everyone I could think of. Didn't you think, Jake? Didn't you realise how worried I'd be?'

She didn't give me time to answer. I sipped the hot soup. Then she asked, 'And where have you been, Jake? Martin's out there now, looking for you.'

'I've seen him,' I said. 'He's coming round by the road. But Mum – ' I hesitated. This was going to hurt her. 'I've been up the mountain again.'

She stared, her face going white.

'I won't do it again,' I promised. 'I've realised it's stupid – and I didn't enjoy it either, letting you down.'

She sat down shakily. 'Oh Jake,' she whispered. 'You promised me – you promised me.'

I went to bed soon after, thinking that the day had been a total mess. Just about everything had gone wrong.

Next morning, we sat around the breakfast table

in silence. Mum was pale, her eyes looking heavy as though she hadn't slept. Holly's eyes were rimmed with red and Martin looked very tired. I was aching in every joint and very sad. Nobody ate much, not even me.

'We can't go to church like this,' Martin said. 'I think we'd better stay at home and talk things out.'

We all nodded, but no one knew how to start. It came to me that we had to talk to God first. So I said, 'Martin, can we pray together – now before anyone says anything?'

Yes, I did! I know it's hard to believe that I'd suggest such a thing – and I said the prayer myself:

'Lord Jesus, please forgive me for being selfish. For a long time I've been thinking only about myself, even though I've wanted to change. I haven't really cared about anyone else, but now I see that I've got to give things up because they make other people unhappy. So, I want to give up trying to get my own way all the time. Help me to change. I know that you want me to work hard to make this family happy. And that's what I want to do now. If only you will help me.'

Mum said, and she was crying, that it was a very good prayer and she wanted to say it for herself too. Martin agreed. 'Living in a family is never easy,' he said. 'It would be a lot easier, though, if we all prayed that every day. Thank you, Jake.'

I wouldn't want you to think that nothing went wrong ever again for us. I still find it hard to think of other people's happiness first, but there was a change after that.

I now felt that we were one family – not two halves. I felt I belonged. You see, I was forgiven completely. Both Mum and Martin knew what I'd done – breaking my promise – but they both said they'd trust me again. I've kept the promise too. I have been up the mountain, though. Martin said I ought to join a club and learn how to climb properly – and I'm enjoying that. And Martin has taken us, the family, right to the top of our mountain and several others. Even Mum's learning to love the mountains again, though I know she thinks of Dad when we're up there. I do. When I'm old enough I'm going to join the Mountain Rescue service. I'll have to break that to Mum gently!

And Holly?

For a while after that Sunday, I couldn't understand her. Things were so much better in the family, but she seemed unhappy. It was she, not me, who was moody and awkward. She seemed to avoid being with me.

One day, I found her hanging around at the end of the back garden. It was the summer holidays. The weather was warm and bright, but she had nothing to do.

'I've told Mum I'm going to the field,' I told her. 'You want to come?'

She shook her head.

'Why not?'

'I don't have to!' she yelled, quite like the old 'Prickly' Holly I'd almost forgotten.

I said, 'Please yourself, then, Prickles,' and went through the fence.

The field was very green after some heavy rain in the night, but now the sun was shining, lighting up the grass and flowers with drops of silver. The air was alive with bird song. The mountain behind was purple with heather.

'Just the day for going to the hide,' I thought and felt a pang of sorrow that it wasn't there any more. What good times Holly and I had shared there!

'She feels like this too,' I thought. 'That's why she won't come into the field. She can't bear to see the gap where the hide was.'

I squeezed back into the garden. Holly was still there, kicking stones. She looked at me and frowned.

'It's not such a big hole in the hedge when you come to look,' I said. 'It's quite small really – only one of those little gates across it. Come and see.'

She shook her head.

'Why not?'

'I don't have to!' she shouted. 'You can't make me, Jake.' What could I do for her? I went back to the house and asked my mother. I started to explain about the hide. You remember that it had been a secret, even from her? Well, I found out that she knew about it already!

'Of course Holly misses it,' she said. 'Perhaps she thinks you won't want her any more now there's no hide to share.'

I walked down the garden, thinking hard.

'Holly,' I said, 'did you tell Mum about the hide?'

She gasped, looking terrified. 'I had to,' she squeaked. 'I told her the day you went missing.

I thought you'd run away because it was being pulled down. I told Sue you'd gone off because of that. I thought it might help them find you.' She was crying. 'I'm sorry, Jake. I know I promised never to tell a living soul, but I had to. Sue was so worried. And Dad was out looking for you. I wanted to help find you. I thought it might help. I'm sorry!'

When I'd broken my promise (and it was much more serious than what Holly had done) I'd been forgiven. So I forgave Holly. Well, what else could I have done? She'd done it for my sake after all.

'Look, Holly,' I said. 'It's all right. Anyway, the hide's gone, so it doesn't matter anyone knowing.'

She smiled, just a little.

'If you come into the field,' I went on, 'we could find another place for a hide, perhaps even better than the last one. We might have to build it ourselves. We could make it further out of the ditch, you know, nearer the field on one side.'

'Could we?'

'Yes,' I told her. 'Mr Grainger left most of the hedge, you know. He was all right in the end, wasn't he?'

She nodded, brushing away her tears. 'Do you really think we could make a new hide?'

'If you help me,' I said. 'I won't do it on my own.'

Light sparkled from her eyes. 'Wait for me, then,' she cried. 'I've got to change out of this dress – and tell Sue we're going out together. This is going to be even better fun!'

I sat on the ground waiting for her.

Do you think God answers prayers? I do. I didn't at first. When I'd been praying that Mum wouldn't get married again, God had said, 'No'.

I smiled. 'I'd have missed so much if Martin and Holly hadn't come to live with us,' I thought. 'God knew best all along.'

Later, my prayers had been answered. I'd prayed to be different, less selfish, and that was happening. I was changing in lots of ways. And I was happier, much happier, because I'd discovered the secret – making other people happy makes you happy too!

Soon, Holly was running towards me, dressed in a new grey track suit, her plaited hair bobbing up and down behind her.

'Come on, Jake,' she cried, dashing past me, 'I can't wait to get started!'